Yellowstone On Fire!

By The Staff Of The Billings Gazette

Story by Robert Ekey

Photos by Larry Mayer, Bob Zellar, James Woodcock and Judy Tell

Billings Gazette
The Source.

The staff of *The Billings Gazette*
Story by Robert Ekey
Photos by Larry Mayer, Bob Zellar, James Woodcock
   and Judy Tell
Graphics by John Potter
Edited by Robert C. Gibson

© 1989 The Billings Gazette

Published by The Billings Gazette.
Wayne Schile, Publisher
Richard J. Wesnick, Editor

Distributed by Falcon Press.

Library of Congress Catalog Card Number 88-63503

ISBN 0-937959-54-5

10 9 8 7 6 5 4 3 2 1

Design: Steve Morehouse
Falcon Press Coordinator: Marnie Hagmann
Design, typesetting and other prepress work by Falcon Press, Helena, Montana. Printed in Korea.

For extra copies of this book

Individuals contact:

The Billings Gazette
P.O. Box 36300
Billings, MT 59107-6300
In Montana 1-800-332-7089
In North Dakota, South Dakota,
Wyoming and Idaho 1-800-325-4298
Elsewhere (406) 657-1200

Book retailers and wholesalers contact:

Falcon Press
318 North Last Chance Gulch
P.O. Box 1718
Helena, MT 59624
1-800-582-BOOK

Front cover: A firestorm moves toward the Norris Geyser Basin on Aug. 20, 1988.
LARRY MAYER

First page: Old Faithful geyser, the most famous tourist attraction in Yellowstone Park, erupts against a smoke-filled sky.
BOB ZELLAR

Title page: The North Fork fire illuminates the night skyline south of West Yellowstone.
LARRY MAYER

Back cover: Stephen Albers, a sawyer on the Clover-Mist fire, stands silhouetted against the glowing flames.
JAMES WOODCOCK

ACKNOWLEDGMENTS

For nearly three months, the staff of *The Billings Gazette* fought a daily race against deadlines, distance and nature to bring news of the Yellowstone Park fires to their readers.

The nearest entrance to Yellowstone is more than 100 miles from Billings but photographers and reporters often traveled three to four times that distance each day.

On some days, the *Gazette* had as many as 12 reporters, photographers and editors in or around the park, covering the fires with an intensity matched only by the blazes themselves.

Special recognition must be given to reporter Patricia Bellinghausen, the first reporter to cover the park fires; reporter Vikki McLaughlin, who wrote fire stories each day for months; and reporter Tom Howard who staffs the *Gazette*'s Cody, Wyo., bureau and who rarely missed a day on the fire lines. Others who contributed greatly to the reporting effort included Jaci Johnson, Dennis Gaub, Roger Clawson, Clair Johnson, Mark Henckel and virtually every other reporter and editor who worked in the park or on copy at the *Gazette*.

Obviously, we would be remiss if we did not applaud the efforts of Chief Photographer Larry Mayer who flew his own plane on 20 round-trips to the park; photographers Bob Zellar, James Woodcock and Judy Tell, and our Bozeman Bureau Reporter Robert Ekey who not only covered the fires daily but who is also the author of this book. Robert Gibson, the *Gazette*'s region editor, served as editor for the text of this book.

Richard J. Wesnick
Editor, *The Billings Gazette*

Above: Days after fire swept along the Madison River, elk return to graze. Wildlife often were seen in recently burned areas seeking mineral-rich ash. BOB ZELLAR

Next page: Flames dance above the treetops as a firestorm sweeps north of the town of Silver Gate. JAMES WOODCOCK

CONTENTS

Early morning smoke blankets the fire camp at Grant Village as firefighters start their day. BOB ZELLAR

INTRODUCTION

Heat has always been the essence of Yellowstone National Park's wonder. The park is home to the world's largest and most spectacular geothermal basin, where heat from the center of the earth mixes with water and pressure, then surfaces in a dramatic display of geysers, fumaroles and hot pools—the release valve for an underground pressure cooker.

Throughout the summer of 1988, heat played another major role for Yellowstone. This time the nation's oldest park was ablaze with massive forest fires.

Record-low snowpack and a near-total absence of rain left the Yellowstone high country parched in late June. Then lightning struck and sparked fires that smoldered through July, when persistent winds fanned them into the infernos of August and September.

The forest was as dry as at any time this century, creating unprecedented burning conditions and fire behavior that surprised even the most experienced firefighters. High winds frequently pushed the fires as fast as 2 miles per hour. Advances of 5 to 10 miles in one day were common. One fire traveled 14 miles in three hours. Smoke billowed 10 miles into the air and blanketed the park with a silent, acrid pall.

Thousands of firefighters mobilized for the largest forest-fire-fighting effort ever. The military joined the forces at the height of the fires. Dozens of helicopters, spotting planes and aerial tankers dotted the skies. For months, Yellowstone more closely resembled a war zone than a tourist mecca.

Firefighters built more than 1,000 miles of fire line and dropped millions of gallons of water and retardant, but the fires seemed only to pause before sweeping forward.

Nearly every development in Yellowstone and most of the communities along its boundaries were threatened by fire. Despite man's best efforts, a dozen fires raged out of control for most of August and September. Only when fall storms cooled the air and dropped snow did the fires subside.

Drought and fire were not limited to Yellowstone National Park. Major fires exploded in national forest wilderness

Bright yellow aspens provide a sharp contrast to the charred areas as fall arrives in the Yellowstone high country.
BOB ZELLAR

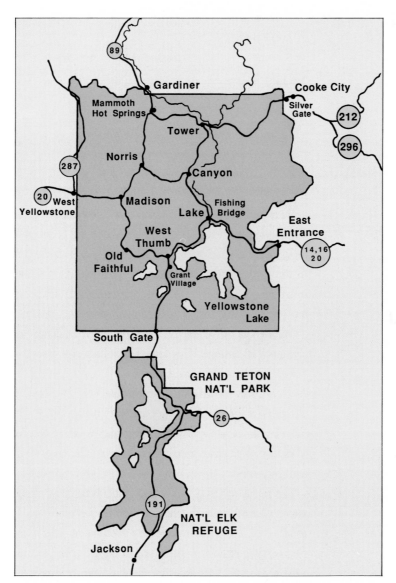

*Forest fires swept across 40 percent of Yellowstone National Park
during the summer of 1988, threatening many developments in the park
and communities along its boundaries.* MAP BY JOHN POTTER

adjacent to the park, forcing federal agencies to combine their efforts.

Fires burned 1.3 million acres in the greater Yellowstone area, including 900,000 acres within Yellowstone Park. The fires burned with varying intensity, creating mosaics in the forest.

Yellowstone's summer of fire also created heat for federal land managers. The firestorm brought to light a federal "let it burn" policy that allowed some lightning-caused fires to burn unchecked early in the summer. Firefighters were not ordered to suppress some of the blazes until late July.

The 17-year-old policy, which also governs wilderness areas, reflects scientists' conclusions that fire is a vital element of the life cycle of Yellowstone, destroying overmature forests and allowing regeneration. Fire has been part of the ecosystem since the glaciers receded 12,000 years ago. According to scientists, it is as necessary as sunshine and rain.

Even before the last flames fizzled, Yellowstone showed signs of new life in the charred ground. Thousands of lodgepole pine seeds, released when the fires popped open their cones, have sprouted from beneath the ashes. Wildflowers and forbs appeared in wet areas just weeks after fire swept through.

The Yellowstone fires tugged at the hearts of people who felt attached to the park. They also provided a lesson in nature's view of the landscape.

*Firefighters scramble to
protect buildings at Old
Faithful when a
firestorm rages over
them.* BOB ZELLAR

SIEGE OF '88

As fire raged through lodgepole pines on the edge of Grant Village in Yellowstone National Park, experienced firefighters stared wide-eyed at the spectacle as they prepared to make their last stand. All non-essential personnel from their nearby fire camp huddled along the shores of Yellowstone Lake, the designated "safe" spot— safe because it was open and people could wade into the frigid waters if necessary to avoid the fire.

The blaze already had overrun all efforts to stop it and the firefighters, poised with their hoses at the edge of the forest, were the village's last defense. Brush had been removed from around buildings that make up the new, $15 million development in the southern end of Yellowstone. Firefighters stood ready to knock the fire out of the trees before it could roar into the hotels, restaurants and shops and their camp.

As the fire approached, hoses went off like cannons aimed at the sky. The firefighters were successful and, within two hours, the fire camp's caterer was serving dinner.

It was a dramatic scene in Yellowstone at the time, something that had never occurred before. But that was early in the 1988 fire season and the sight of firefighters working feverishly to save towns would be repeated dozens of times in August and September, until fall snows doused the fires.

By the time the historic fire season ended, fires scorched 900,000 acres of Yellowstone National Park and 400,000 acres of adjacent national forests. The flames swept across the drought-ridden region despite a $120 million effort which, at its peak, included 9,500

Firefighter Jill Jayne stares at the flames of the Red fire burning near Lewis Lake in southern Yellowstone.

BOB ZELLAR

firefighters, 117 aircraft and more than 100 fire engines from throughout the country. Two people died and hundreds more suffered minor injuries and fire-related illness.

Yellowstone's fire problems started early in the summer. On June 23, a lone bolt of lightning touched off the Shoshone fire in the southern end of the park. Two days later, the Fan fire was spotted in the north-western corner of the park and, within a week, the Red fire started near the Shoshone.

Park rangers watched Yellowstone's fires early in the summer, but allowed them to burn under what became known as the "let it burn" policy. During 15 years under that policy—which allows natural wildfires to burn as long as they do not threaten life or property —only 34,000 acres had burned in the park.

The Shoshone fire burned 160 acres during its first 30 days. During the second week of July, the total area of burned land in the park doubled. That week the Shoshone and Red fires burned toward each other. The Clover and Mist fires were burning in the eastern end of the park. The fire season was in full swing with a sudden increase in the size and numbers of fires.

On July 22, the Shoshone fire exploded to 1,000 acres. By the end of the next day, it was 4,500 acres

and on July 26 it roared to the edge of Grant Village.

July 22 also was a bad day outside Yellowstone. Someone gathering firewood in the Targhee National Forest in Idaho accidentally started a fire within 200 yards of the park's western boundary. The blaze quickly spread into the park and became the North Fork fire, one of the most frustrating and damaging fires of the season.

The extreme burning conditions—downed logs in the forest had less moisture than kiln-dried lumber—prompted park officials to begin full suppression. All new fire starts would be aggressively attacked and firefighters would work to contain the fires

Above: Scores of fire crews respond to a call to help defend buildings at Grant Village.
LARRY MAYER

Right: An aerial view shows fire encroaching on Grant Village, one of Yellowstone's largest tourist developments.
LARRY MAYER

already burning out of control.

Weather and landscape always are factors in forest fires. Ironically, Yellowstone's magnificent landscape contributed heavily to the intensity of fire during the summer of 1988. The park's deeply glaciated, high-elevation mountains give way to flat plateaus and broad valleys covered with dense lodgepole pine forests and crossed by few roads. The expanses of forest, devoid of prominent breaks or access, hampered firefighting efforts.

While the landscape played a role, weather was the critical difference in 1988. The region started drying out in the fall of 1987 when seasonal rains failed to materialize. A record-low snowpack and early spring runoff aggravated the situation to the point that even spring rain did not help. By mid-June, a scientific analysis of precipitation, soil moisture and evaporation showed that the Yellowstone region was in the grips of extreme drought. When high-speed, warm winds joined the scene, it set the stage for the worst fire season in the park's history.

Yellowstone, designated the world's first national park in 1872, occupies 2.2 million acres of high country in northwestern Wyoming and southern Montana. But it is not an island of wild lands. It is surrounded by Grand Teton National Park and six national forests that share similar topography and wildlife to make up the greater Yellowstone ecosystem.

Fires in the Yellowstone area in 1988 crossed boundaries between national parks and forests as easily as elk on their winter migration. The U.S. Forest Service and Park Service, which manage the land, worked together to coordinate the fire-suppression effort. Trained fire-management teams set up a command post in the small town of West Yellowstone to disburse firefighters, equipment and supplies and to coordinate the effort. Firefighting teams were composed mostly of experienced Forest Service workers.

As the fire encroached on Grant Village, guests and employees were asked to leave. But dozens of reporters flocked to the scene. Yellowstone is dear to the hearts of millions of people, and any activity there draws greater attention than a similar event elsewhere.

A few days after the Shoshone fire swept to the edge of Grant Village, the North Fork fire began a run toward Old Faithful. Although the fire was six miles away, firefighters were assigned to Old Faithful to protect the historic log inn and other buildings around the famous geyser. Even the distant threat of fire at Old Faithful drew more national attention than actual

flames at Grant Village. That attention shed considerable public light on the "let it burn" policy.

Interior Secretary Donald Hodel visited the park on July 27 and expressed support for Yellowstone's fire management policy. Before Hodel's visit, the fires in Yellowstone had burned fewer than 50,000 acres—less than 2 percent of the park. When Hodel returned to Yellowstone in September, on a fact-finding mission for President Ronald Reagan, fires in the greater Yellowstone area were approaching 1 million acres. He announced later that the fire management policy would get a thorough review.

When Hodel first visited the park, extensive firefighting efforts already were under way. Helicopters dropped burning Ping-Pong-size balls of fuel in the

Previous page: Firefighter Clyde Johnson watches as the Red fire approaches the Lewis Lake campground. BOB ZELLAR

Above: Flames leap up tree trunks near Grant Village, evidence of the tinder-dry conditions in the forested areas. BOB ZELLAR

Right: A helicopter dips water from Crazy Creek to drop on the Clover-Mist fire. Helicopters dropped 10 million gallons of water in the greater Yellowstone area. BOB ZELLAR

forests in front of the North Fork fire. The burning balls started small fires, which were sucked toward the larger blaze. This was designed to eradicate fuel and leave the North Fork fire nothing to burn.

But Yellowstone's 1988 fires frustrated such traditional firefighting techniques. In a phenomenon known as ''spotting,'' heavy winds lifted hot embers above the treetops and deposited them beyond fire lines and backfires, starting new fires.

Despite the extreme fire activity, most firefighters and park officials remained optimistic that they could stop the flames. One exception was Larry Caplinger, incident commander of the North Fork fire. As early as July 27, he said, ''We could be in for the beginning of the Siege of 1988.''

Firefighters employed some of the latest technology available to fight the fires. Infrared maps of the park were made during high-altitude nighttime flights and handed to fire commanders the next morning so they could monitor fire progress and plot their strategy. Helicopters and air tankers dropped water and flame retardant on the leading edges of the fires. But firefighters also used some of the oldest technology available to fight the fires. Teams of pack horses and mules hauled supplies to ''spike camps'' in the backcountry where firefighters slept on the ground.

Early firefighting efforts were fruitless and the fires intensified daily. The unprecedented, persistent winds continued to fan the fires and aggravate the dry conditions. Strategy changed from building containment lines in front of some fires to narrowing the fire front by pinching the flanks.

A team of fire-behavior experts arrived in West Yellowstone late in July to predict where the fires would burn by the end of August. While they were experienced in predicting fire growth in terms of days, this was the first attempt at predicting fire growth for an entire month.

The experts worked for two days studying historical weather patterns, fire behavior and the ages of the forests in the path of the fires. They fed the information into computers and, during the first days of August, presented their predictions to fire commanders and Park Service and Forest Service officials.

They used large maps of the fire perimeters with clear plastic overlays to predict where the fires would be on Aug. 15 and Aug. 31. But, even as they made their presentation to a meeting of officials at West Yellowstone on Aug. 2, the perimeters of some fires were burning past the Aug. 15 prediction lines.

The fires had made major runs while the prediction team still was feeding data into computers. The projections said the fires, which encompassed 125,000 acres, would grow by 25 to 50 percent in 30 days. Within five days, the fires had exceeded the acreage projections for the end of the month.

The Fan fire in the northwestern corner of the park was making a mad dash toward the northern park boundary, threatening to spill over onto private lands owned by the Church Universal and Triumphant (CUT), an eclectic religious sect which has its international headquarters on a sprawling ranch north of Yellowstone. CUT followers annually gather near the park on a parcel of land they call the "Heart of the Inner Retreat." Church officials threatened to sue the National Park Service if the fire swept through their sacred religious grounds.

Meanwhile, sect leader Elizabeth Clare Prophet,

Above: Crews walk between hot spots along the fire line. Breathing the dense smoke is the equivalent of smoking four packs of cigarettes a day. JAMES WOODCOCK

Right: Fanned by high winds, fire sweeps up to the edge of Grant Village in late July. The development was saved when firefighters used hoses to knock the flames out of the trees. LARRY MAYER

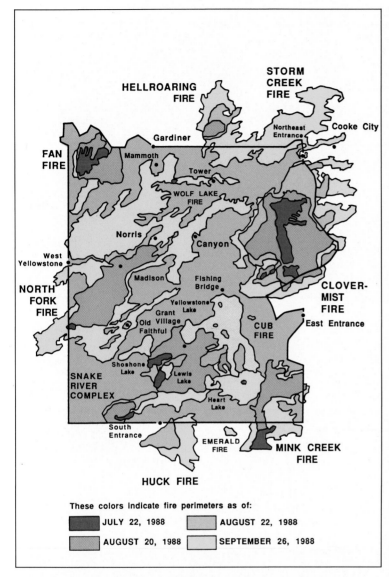

HELLROARING
FIRE

STORM
CREEK
FIRE

Gardiner

Northeast
Entrance

Cooke City

FAN
FIRE

Mammoth

Tower

WOLF LAKE
FIRE

Norris

Canyon

West
Yellowstone

NORTH
FORK
FIRE

Madison

Fishing
Bridge

CLOVER-
MIST
FIRE

Yellowstone
Lake

East Entrance

Grant
Village

Old
Faithful

CUB
FIRE

SNAKE
RIVER
COMPLEX

Shoshone
Lake

Lewis
Lake

Heart
Lake

South
Entrance

EMERALD
FIRE

MINK CREEK
FIRE

HUCK FIRE

These colors indicate fire perimeters as of:

■ JULY 22, 1988		■ AUGUST 22, 1988	
■ AUGUST 20, 1988		□ SEPTEMBER 26, 1988	

This map shows the fires' progress throughout the summer in four stages. The first stage shows the scope of the fires on July 22, when firefighting efforts began on all fires. Aug. 20 was Black Saturday, when high winds fanned fires to new dimensions. The outside outline shows the final fire perimeters. MAP BY JOHN POTTER

*Employees of TW
Services, the park's
major concessionaire,
wait to be evacuated
from Grant Village.*
JAMES WOODCOCK.

Firefighters rest after
spending hours building
fire lines, the grueling
job of clearing trails
through the forest in an
effort to stop the fire.
LARRY MAYER

whom followers call "Guru Ma," led 250 church members to a meadow near the encroaching fire, where they shouted high-speed chants to try to reverse the fire's spread. In a rapid-fire monotone unintelligible to an unpracticed ear, the members chanted, "Reverse the tide. Roll them back. Set all free." Firefighters already had stepped up their efforts along the park boundary near the CUT ranch, attacking the fire with additional crews and aircraft. Keeping fire off private property was a high priority.

The night after the CUT members chanted, the fire activity subsided and firefighters were able to hold the containment line along the boundary. Both firefighters and CUT members claimed credit for one of man's few successes against Yellowstone's 1988 fires.

CUT officials joined other residents of the region in assailing the National Park Service for initially allowing the fires to burn. Although the Park Service had said it was trying to put all the fires out as of July 22, many in the region continued to complain about the policy.

The fires were beginning to affect the tourism trade. Residents of smoke-choked gateway communities were

Left: A mountain of provisions surrounds a firefighter at the West Yellowstone supply camp. Supplying the thousands of firefighters was a logistical challenge.
JAMES WOODCOCK

Above: Scott Park uses his pulaski to put out a spot fire near Grant Village. Pulaskis, hand tools which are a combination hoe and axe, are the firefighter's primary tool. LARRY MAYER

upset that a tourist season which had shown promise was dwindling. Road closures created an obstacle course for tourist traffic.

Other tourists were fascinated by the fires. They listened to Park Service naturalists talk about the role fire plays in the ecology of high-country forests. They snapped pictures and watched firefighting activity as if it were a regular attraction.

Firefighters, meanwhile, reported horror stories from the fire lines on just how tinder-dry the forests were becoming. In one case, a downed log in the southern portion of the park was lit with a single match as part of a backburn. One firefighter said he watched as fire crept along the ground until it came to a standing lodgepole. Within 30 seconds, the entire tree was engulfed in flames.

Dave Poncin, who was incident commander when the Red-Shoshone fire invaded Grant Village, was

called back to oversee the North Fork fire in mid-August. He reported that, in the three weeks since he was first called to Yellowstone, fire conditions had grown much more extreme. Meadows which once acted as barriers to fires had turned from green to brown and were now carrying flames.

During mid-August, the North Fork fire swept around Madison Junction and jumped the Firehole, Gibbon and Madison rivers in one day, closing roads in the area. The fire prediction team had said that the fire would not reach Madison Junction by the end of the month.

One member of the fire prediction team said later that the projections underestimated the fire's spread for several reasons. Fires were burning through all kinds of vegetation, including younger lodgepole stands that were not expected to carry the fires. The team also had not anticipated the unseasonable, unrelenting, high winds which fanned the fires. Later, other fire-behavior specialists working the fires doubled and quadrupled their projections to take into account the extremely dry conditions.

Extreme fire behavior was not limited to the park. On Aug. 16, Yellowstone's Assistant Superintendent Ben Clary and Chief Ranger Dan Sholly were on a helicopter reconnaissance flight over the north end of the park when they spotted a new fire burning in the Absaroka-Beartooth Wilderness of the Gallatin National Forest. The helicopter landed and Clary and Sholly worked to save an outfitter's camp next to where

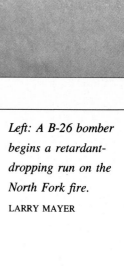

Previous page: The Clover-Mist fire casts an eerie glow by moonlight with Pilot Peak in the background.
BOB ZELLAR

Left: A B-26 bomber begins a retardant-dropping run on the North Fork fire.
LARRY MAYER

Manning a shovel, a firefighter runs through a meadow to extinguish a spot fire. BOB ZELLAR

the fire was burning. They radioed for help and smoke-jumpers were flown to the scene, but could not parachute to the ground because of high winds.

Sholly and Clary manned shovels, but the fire grew too quickly. Within a day it covered 250 acres and, before the end of a week, had grown to more than 2,000 acres. The Hellroaring fire was born.

Meanwhile the Clover-Mist fire in the northeast corner of the park was pressing its way toward the Montana communities of Cooke City and Silver Gate. Residents accused the Park Service of taking inadequate action to stop the fire, then about 10 miles away. ''Nobody likes to play with fire,'' one resident said.

As the fire activity grew, the face of Yellowstone changed. Campgrounds once occupied by recreational vehicles and tourists' tents became fire camps where firefighters slept and fire bosses planned and coordinated strategy. Caterers served thousands of meals to famished firefighters. Showers and portable telephones were brought to these impromptu cities. Computers in the back of cargo vans tracked the logistics of caring for fire crews.

The air over Yellowstone suddenly was full of helicopters and airplanes—a mainstay in forest firefighting efforts since the end of World War II. Heliports to service the dozens of helicopters popped up in open meadows where elk and bison usually graze.

The plethora of aircraft caused safety problems. Fire bosses threatened to shut down all air traffic in August after two incidents in which pilots had to take evasive action to miss other aircraft. They blamed the problems on pilots using different radio frequencies.

Fire bosses also preached safety to the firefighters on the ground, who had to take special precautions because of Yellowstone's special circumstances. Crews working in the park's backcountry had to keep an eye out for grizzly bears. They stored their garbage in bear-proof traps and flew it out of the area daily. A half-dozen firefighters were treated at a Yellowstone clinic after they inhaled sulfur gas while working around a hot spring. Other crews walked cautiously around thermal areas to keep from breaking through the thin crust next to hot pools.

By Aug. 19, the fires' perimeters had spread over 282,000 acres. The ranks of firefighters had grown to more than 2,000. Firefighters were meeting little success and said their only hope for gaining was rain, which hadn't fallen in a month, or a break in the wind. But relief did not arrive. In fact, the worst was yet to come.

*Skies hazy with smoke
created spectacular
sunsets, such as this
one near Grant Village.*
JAMES WOODCOCK

BLACK SATURDAY

Midnight approached on Aug. 19 as photographer Larry Mayer and I stood near Beryl Hot Springs, in the Gibbon Canyon between Madison Junction and Norris. The spring belched a sulfur-laden mist into air already heavy with wood smoke from hundreds of small fires that dotted the canyon walls.

An arm of the North Fork fire had swept through the area earlier in the day as it headed north toward Norris. After the winds died down and the temperature dropped, the fire was reduced to the spots glowing around us, many the size of campfires, some still as big as 20 feet in diameter. Occasionally flames flared through a patch of small trees, only to lie back down again, as if rousing in their sleep.

The fires sleeping on that Friday night awakened on Saturday morning to a high wind that quickly slapped them into action. By noon, the small, seemingly harmless camp-fires joined and grew into a monster with flames 200 feet tall, sweeping toward Norris in an angry firestorm hungry for more fuel to maintain its fierce existence.

Mother Nature flexed her muscles that morning. Winds sustained themselves at 30 to 40 miles per hour and gusted to 70 miles per hour. Trees blew down and fires grew so fierce that they created their own wind. Mammoth flames reached far above the treetops and arched with the wind, like a giant wave ready to crash down on the forest below.

By midmorning, the strong winds grounded helicopters and airplanes. The fires grew so intense that all attempts to slow them were futile. Firefighters could work only

Gale-force winds whipped flames to a frenzy on Aug. 20— Black Saturday—the worst single day of fire activity in the summer of 1988. BOB ZELLAR

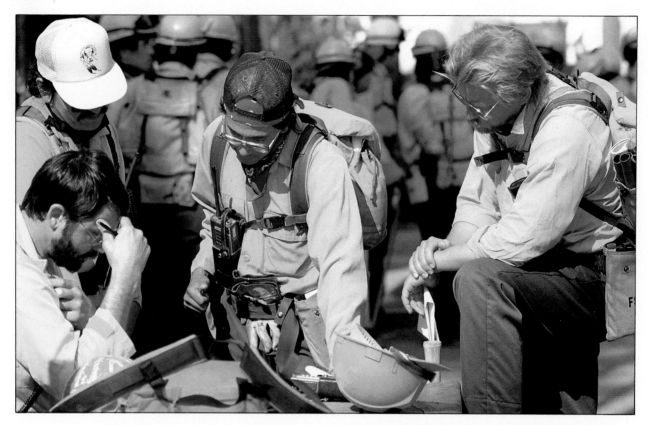

in a few isolated areas to protect buildings—and helplessly watch the roaring fires.

Weather forecasters had predicted a "red-flag day" that Saturday with winds faster than 20 miles per hour, hot temperatures and low humidity. But the weather and its results surprised even the most experienced firefighters. They never had seen so much sustained wind in a wildfire.

By midnight of Aug. 20—dubbed "Black Saturday"—fires throughout the Yellowstone region had consumed an additional 165,000 acres of forest land, growing by more than 50 percent in a single day. Every fire in the area made major runs. Fires which had been smoldering sprang to life and new starts quickly became major fires. Black Saturday forever changed firefighters' perceptions of fire activity in the Yellowstone region. They realized the futility of trying to stop fires at their fronts and just how explosive fire conditions were.

The intense fire caused chaos in Yellowstone. Roads closed, stranding tourists. Dozens of firefighters had to flee the flames.

Yellowstone Superintendent Robert Barbee attended a meeting at West Yellowstone that morning and later found the direct route back to park headquarters in Mammoth closed by fire. He took the roundabout route and ran into more fire. In midafternoon Barbee found himself at West Thumb in south-central Yellowstone, helping rangers hastily evacuate tourists as the Red-Shoshone fire made a run at the development.

Similar scenes were played out throughout the greater Yellowstone region that day. Fires crossed roads, separating tourists from their hotel rooms. Travelers dashed along roads past uncontrolled wildfire to escape from the park's flaming interior.

The fires would have other hot days, but none that saw fires grow as quickly as on Black Saturday. "On Saturday, we could have had the entire United States

Above: Frustrated fire bosses huddle to discuss strategy as fires continue to sweep across fire lines and ignore man's attempts to slow them.
JAMES WOODCOCK

Right: Firefighters hose down the roof of the Norris Museum. They feared the fires would shower embers on the shake roof.
LARRY MAYER

Army in here and it wouldn't have made any difference,'' Barbee said.

Mayer, *The Billings Gazette*'s chief photographer, and I spent the day with firefighters watching the North Fork fire. Fire officials had anticipated an active day, but were caught by surprise when the winds kicked up well before noon. A planned 1 p.m. closure of the highway inside the western edge of the park that links Norris and Madison Junction was quickly moved up and rangers in patrol cars used loudspeakers to hustle tourists out of the area.

Near Elk Park, fire swept through treetops and threatened to cross the highway. We moved north of the fire, toward Norris, and stood with fire officials watching the inferno, vehicles idling in the roadway. Wind gusts to 60 miles per hour snapped trees in the forest around us. Thick, gray smoke was pouring over our heads as we watched and waited.

As it nears, a wildfire creates much the same sensation as an approaching train. First one hears—almost feels—a distant rumble. Puffs of black smoke appear in the columns of gray—a sign of greater burning intensity—and the sound of the fire increases. Then whiffs of air hit the back of your neck as you face the fire, evidence that the fire is creating its own wind, sucking oxygen from along the ground to sustain itself, then blowing it thousands of feet into the air in a boiling column of smoke.

As the inferno nears, it roars like a jet engine as the blaze sucks more and more air. You can feel the heat and see the flames half a mile away. Thick smoke occasionally obscures the blaze and the noise dissipates for a moment as the flames gasp momentarily for air before making their next leap.

Man always has regarded fire, in its undisciplined form, as evil and destructive. But the unbridled fury of wildfire raging through a forest also creates a sense of awe and a fascination for nature at work.

As we stood with a dozen fire officials on Black Saturday, southwesterly winds pushed the roaring blaze along the roadway past us. A quick shift in the wind direction suddenly brought the flames directly toward the group and sent people scrambling for their vehicles. Even inside the vehicles, the heat was as intense as if someone had left the car heater on in the middle of summer.

Through thick smoke that cut visibility to 25 yards, the group eased northward toward Norris, listening for the telltale roar, feeling for the heat and peering into the grayness for the dark-orange glow that would tell us that the fire was near.

At Norris, a dozen firefighters and rangers gathered to try to protect the historic log museum that overlooks the geyser basins there. The steaming, barren geyser basins stood as a substantial barrier between the museum and the raging fire, but firefighters worried that a thin band of trees could carry the fire close enough to drop embers on the museum's shake roof. A pair of firefighters hosed down the roof of the small museum building while the others took up positions near the forest and prepared to knock the approaching flames out of the treetops.

As the inevitable inferno approached, flames 200 feet tall burned to within 150 yards of the museum. The heat, even through the dense smoke and steam from geysers, was searing. Above the approaching roar came what sounded like rifle shots as trees exploded in the intense heat. Rangers took bearings on barren ''safe spots'' in the geyser basin in case they needed to flee from the fire.

Firefighters are trained to keep a safe spot in mind at all times and go there if a fire overtakes them. In addition, they wear flame-retardant clothing and carry fire shelters—thick, foil, one-person tents they can crawl into to escape a fire. Firefighters learn to lie on barren ground and pull the shelter over themselves. People who have used fire shelters say they can get hot enough to burn flesh, so firefighters wear gloves to protect their hands as they pull the tents over their heads.

Though firefighters call the shelters "brown-and-serve bags," they are credited with saving dozens of lives. During the 1988 Yellowstone fires, more than four dozen people deployed fire shelters.

There was no need to use the fire shelters at Norris

Left: Flames shoot hundreds of feet above the trees as a firestorm sweeps forward, generating its own wind and weather.

BOB ZELLAR

Above: A firefighter douses a spot fire near the Norris Museum caused when high winds carried burning embers miles ahead of a firestorm.

LARRY MAYER

Previous page:
Hundreds of small fires
smolder along the
Gibbon River on the
eve of Black Saturday.
The next day, wind
whipped the fires into a
firestorm. LARRY MAYER

Above: Fire bosses
monitor the North Fork
fire as it rages along
the highway south of
Norris on Black
Saturday. Thousands of
acres went up in smoke
that day. LARRY MAYER

on Black Saturday. The fire stopped at the edge of the geyser basin. Another finger of flames later ran past Norris and burned toward other developments.

The gale-force winds of Black Saturday pushed glowing embers forward and spotting, like all other fire activity, was at its worst. On Black Saturday, airborne embers landed as far as a mile and a half ahead of the fires. The embers started fires with incredible frequency—in some instances every time one landed. With fuel moisture levels and humidity at record lows and temperatures in the 80s, the spots smoldered only minutes before bursting into flames.

The spot fires grew in size as they were pulled toward the main fire by fire-induced drafts. Continuing to grow in size and intensity, they drew the main fire toward themselves, creating a pulsating action between the two fires, causing both to intensify. When the fires eventually joined, they released even more energy. The proliferation of spot fires created dangerous situations for firefighters who had to be cautious not to get trapped between two fires.

Until Aug. 20, fire officials generally could count on fires burning most actively in the late afternoon, after the sun warmed the air and relative humidity dropped. As evening approached and temperatures fell, the fires would lie down for the night.

On the evening of Black Saturday it was obvious that the fires were not about to lie down. Mayer and I decided to leave Norris before the fast-moving fires cut off the only remaining escape route to Mammoth. Already, it had closed two roads behind us. We also knew that the spectacular fire activity we witnessed that afternoon was not limited just to the Norris area.

As we drove north toward Mammoth, the smoke cleared, revealing huge cumulus clouds perched atop towering smoke columns to the east and northeast, signs that the Hellroaring, Storm Creek and Clover-Mist fires also had exploded that day. To the south, above Norris, the smoke from which we emerged pushed up to 30,000 feet, obliterating from view other smoke columns where new fires had started south of Yellowstone.

Just south of the Yellowstone boundary, wind had pushed a tree across a power line, sparking fire in a thick lodgepole pine stand littered with downed timber. The fire grew 4,000 acres in just two hours—testimony to the extreme burning conditions that day. Called the Huck fire, it expanded so rapidly that

*Standing against a
flame-colored sky,
Yellowstone Park
officials discuss the
intense fire activity of
Black Saturday.*
LARRY MAYER

rangers had to move quickly to evacuate the Flagg Ranch and clear the J.D. Rockefeller Parkway, linking Yellowstone to Grand Teton National Park to the south. The fire roared toward Yellowstone National Park.

At 2 p.m. an aspen tree blew over a power line starting the Hunter fire in Grand Teton National Park. By 8:30 that night the fire had charred 2,000 acres.

The Clover-Mist fire, in the wilderness along Yellowstone's eastern boundary, burned an additional 55,000 acres on Black Saturday as it raced toward Cooke City. Its huge column of smoke spooked residents of the picturesque tourist town, many of whom made plans to evacuate.

The Hellroaring fire, which had started several days before north of Yellowstone in the Absaroka-Beartooth Wilderness area, lived up to its name that day, running an average of one mile per hour for eight hours.

Northeast of Yellowstone, the Storm Creek fire, also in the Absaroka-Beartooth Wilderness, had been smoldering for weeks. On Black Saturday it made an astonishing 10-mile run—astonishing because of its size and because it ran south, against the prevailing winds

---

Above: Firefighters built more than 850 miles of fire lines in the greater Yellowstone area during the summer of 1988. Only a few miles successfully held back the flames.
LARRY MAYER

Right: Black Saturday's fire activity filled the sky with huge smoke columns often capped with thunderheads. The smoke dropped ash on communities as far as 100 miles away.
LARRY MAYER

*Tourists race to beat
flames that were
threatening to jump the
road south of Norris.
Roads closed by fire
often disrupted tourist
traffic.* LARRY MAYER

and in the opposite direction of all the other fires.

The Storm Creek fire, which had burned only 5,500 acres since it started in mid-June, ballooned to 23,680 acres. Fire behavior specialists were puzzled that the Storm Creek fire moved against the prevailing winds. One expert speculated that the fire was drawn south by winds generated by the huge Clover-Mist fire, 10 miles away. Other specialists contended that the prevailing wind reversed itself after crossing a high ridge, creating an eddy of air which swept the fire south.

The Storm Creek fire's advance toward Cooke City narrowed the isthmus of unburned timber surrounding the tiny Montana town at Yellowstone's northeast gate. But residents did not realize the Storm Creek fire had charged toward them from the north. They were preoccupied with the thundering tower of smoke that spread over their mountain community from the Clover-Mist fire to the southwest.

For days, residents of Cooke City and nearby Silver Gate had complained that the Clover-Mist fire threatened them. But Yellowstone officials continued to assure them that the blaze would be contained. On Black Saturday, the Clover-Mist fire ran to within four miles of the communities, held back only by a high ridge.

Charred embers from the Clover-Mist fire dropped into Cooke City as residents wondered whether the fire would stop at the ridge or run into their tourist town, laden with old log buildings.

Smoke exhaled by the Yellowstone fires on Black Saturday sent giant plumes across northern Wyoming, southern Montana and into the Midwest. Ash fell on Billings, 60 miles northeast of the fires. It took little skill to interpret the smoke signals: The Yellowstone fires had entered a new dimension.

More than any other day in the summer of 1988, Black Saturday forced firefighters to change the way they looked at fire. Traditional strategies and tactics were obsolete. Nature was at work and was prevailing.

Frames of reference changed. In one day, nearly five times as much acreage burned in Yellowstone as the previous 16 years combined.

Startled by the day's events, park officials and fire bosses put out a call for help. Additional top-level fire-management teams were summoned to oversee efforts at the Clover-Mist, Hunter, Storm Creek and Hellroaring fires.

Dozens of additional 20-man crews were called in. More helicopters and air tankers were requested. Fire managers met until after midnight to assess the day's events and map new strategy. Those who slept at all arose before dawn to brief fire crews.

Yellowstone's top officials also met until nearly midnight on Black Saturday debating whether to close the park. Tourists had been exposed to wildfire or stranded when fire closed roads between them and their hotel reservations. The officials decided to close the interior of the park until fires subsided. Tourists could see Old Faithful if they entered from West Yellowstone, but travel elsewhere in the park was limited.

Before Black Saturday, park employees already had put in a month of long hours trying to safely mix tourism and the firefighting effort. Frayed nerves and fatigue already were beginning to show.

Late that night, there was a sense of realization among everyone in Yellowstone that the fire season was far from over. In fact, it had just begun on a far grander scale than anyone had ever fathomed.

There would be more red-flag days, more wind and many more acres burned. A quarter-million acres would burn in three days. Fire officials would be forced to direct their limited resources at protecting buildings, leaving other wildfires to burn.

The nightmare, it seemed, had only begun.

Above: Nature's awesome, unbridled fury humbled firefighters for more than three months.

BOB ZELLAR

Next page: On some days smoke was so dense at the West Yellowstone airport that aircraft were grounded.

LARRY MAYER

A NIGHTMARE THAT WOULDN'T END

In the wake of Black Saturday, forest fires swept unchecked across the greater Yellowstone area as firefighters mounted a massive effort. Firefighters from as far away as Hawaii and Florida were called to the Yellowstone high country. The military was called in to supplement civilian crews and the first U.S. Army infantry troops arrived on Aug. 22.

Weather was the firefighters' nemesis, as constant winds sent wildfires sprinting across the parched landscape. Forest Service rangers manned helicopters and rode horses into the backcountry to evacuate people from the path of approaching fire.

Inversions became a daily occurrence, shrouding the park and gateway communities in a blanket of acrid smoke each morning. Adding to the atmosphere of gloom, convoys of civilian and Army firefighters shuttled across the park. With the troops moving to the battle lines and constant helicopter and airplane traffic, Yellowstone more closely resembled a war zone than the nation's premier national park.

As tourism dwindled, the park's concessionaire closed the Lake Hotel. Fire did not threaten the Lake development yet, but thick smoke blocked the view across Yellowstone Lake. Tourists went to bed breathing the smoke and awoke each morning breathing an even stronger stench. Park officials warned tourists with respiratory problems to reconsider their vacation plans.

Like the pall of smoke which covered the park, a sense of frustration and fatalism hung in the air. The massive firefighting effort seemed futile in the face of nature's rage.

A fireball explodes skyward after a dry hillside erupts in flames east of Cooke City.
JAMES WOODCOCK

"It's a nightmare that won't end," one Park Service employee said.

Fires spread despite natural barriers or sparse fuels. Daily fire advances were measured in miles and thousands of acres. The North Fork fire had swept past Norris and its 200-foot-tall flames lapped at the edge of Canyon Village, forcing the evacuation of tourists. Cooke City and Silver Gate, at the park's northeastern corner, were spared by the Clover-Mist fire, but the Storm Creek fire to the north loomed over the tiny mountain communities.

Fire officials compared the fires to the "Big Blowup" of 1910, when a giant wildfire burned 3 million acres of Idaho and Montana forests in 48 hours.

No significant rain had fallen on the Yellowstone area since early July, and the fire conditions worsened.

U.S. Army infantry troops arrive in Bozeman. They were the first of 4,400 soldiers and marines flown in to fight the fires. LARRY MAYER

Throughout the northern Rocky Mountains and the Pacific Northwest, major fires burned. In Yellowstone, the number of firefighters approached 9,000, but the Interagency Fire Center in Boise, Idaho, wanted as many as 1,000 of them and some aircraft to fight other fires. At an Aug. 26 meeting of fire bosses for the 11 major fires burning in the Yellowstone area, forest supervisors and park officials argued that they could not spare crews.

Ultimately, more military, supervised by experienced firefighters, were assigned to relieve civilian crews in Yellowstone.

The extreme burning conditions prompted a significant change in strategy. Firefighters' priorities shifted to containing three small fires which already were under control. New fires were aggressively attacked. Efforts to stop the larger fires head-on became secondary to protecting communities. Backcountry fires that did not threaten buildings were allowed to run their courses.

The changes in strategy marked a change in outlook. Fire bosses no longer were optimistic that they could contain the blazes. Fire-behavior specialists offered worst-case scenarios and made the first projections that the fires could spread to more than 1 million acres—half of Yellowstone National Park.

The moisture level of some logs fell to 7 percent— nearly half that of kiln-dried lumber. Brush, grasses and twigs were measured at 3 percent and 5 percent moisture. At between 8 percent and 12 percent moisture, fires burn freely. Young vegetation burned with ease, something never before witnessed in the region.

Fire officials were disturbed that fuel moisture levels did not rise at night. Normally, as temperature drops at night the relative humidity rises and the forest absorbs moisture from the air. Fires usually burn most intensely during the late afternoon, when fuel is dried by the sun. During Yellowstone's summer of fire, the fuel moisture levels remained low around the clock. Crown fires at midnight left an ominous orange glow in the sky. Firefighting was suspended at night because of the danger.

Dry cold fronts periodically passed through the area, preceded by two days of high winds. Radical fire behavior became a daily occurrence.

Areas within Yellowstone created their own microclimates. Winds blowing southward, up the Grand Canyon of the Yellowstone and against the prevailing wind direction, frustrated firefighters trying to protect Canyon Village.

Nighttime downslope winds pushed the North Fork fire closer to West Yellowstone, against the daytime prevailing winds. The downslope winds, caused by the air cooling at higher elevations in the heart of Yellowstone and drifting down from the high plateau, also brought smoke that hung in the air until midday.

Smoke plumes drifting from fires on the western side of Yellowstone shaded the eastern half of the park, dropping temperatures and substantially reducing fire activity there.

On the rare still days, the fires created their own wind and expanded in all directions, sometimes breaking through fire lines that had held for weeks.

In late August, the southern flank of the North Fork fire broke over a containment line that had held for a month, and renewed its threat to Old Faithful. Although it still was eight miles away from the world-famous geyser basin, winds pushed the fire through dense forests of lodgepole pines killed by mountain bark pine beetles. Dave Poncin, incident commander of the North Fork fire, called the fire's renewed vigor "humbling"—something he hadn't seen before. By then, however, fire bosses were growing accustomed to expecting the unusual.

Fire behavior was so unprecedented that firefighting guidelines were rewritten. Firefighters' perceptions of forest fires changed as well. One 15,000-acre blowup across fire lines on the North Fork fire was called a "slopover." Flanks and rears of fires became fire fronts. Five- and 10-mile advances of fires in one day were predicted and expected. Fires easily jumped the gaping Grand Canyon of the Yellowstone and the barren Old Faithful geyser basin.

As the end of August approached, fire bosses had to lobby the command center for more resources. Commanders had to fight to keep other fires in the nation from siphoning off their men and equipment.

William Penn Mott, director of the National Park

Left: Two firefighters prepare to spray the roof of the historic Old Faithful Inn as fire threatens the area. Nearly 700 guests in the inn were told to leave earlier that day.
JUDY TELL

Above: A Yellowstone employee helps confused tourists route their trip through the park when the fires forced the closure of many developments and roads. LARRY MAYER

*TW Services employee
Sue Harn shields her
face from flying ash
and embers as the
firestorm hits the Old
Faithful complex.*
JUDY TELL

Service, toured Yellowstone and said he was surprised by the extent of the fires. They had burned 660,000 acres in the Yellowstone area, with about two-thirds of that in the national park. Fire commanders told Mott that another dry cold front would move across the area soon, sparking more wind and more extreme fire activity.

The next day high winds sent fires across containment lines again and the perimeters of fires grew to surround 20 percent of the park. The North Fork fire became so large that the commanders divided supervision of efforts against it into two camps. The northeastern half of the fire was renamed the Wolf Lake fire.

Left: A helicopter drops water on fires sweeping toward Silver Gate.
JAMES WOODCOCK

Above: Fireman Dan Bell hoses down a Cooke City cafe as part of an all-out effort to save the town.
JAMES WOODCOCK

Burning south of Canyon and near Hayden Valley, in the center of Yellowstone National Park, the Wolf Lake fire jumped the Yellowstone River and began burning toward the Clover-Mist fire, which had roared across the park's eastern boundary and into the Shoshone National forest, forcing evacuation of two ranches along the Clarks Fork River.

As September approached, firefighters battled a new enemy--fatigue. Some crews were on the fire lines for weeks with little relief. Fire bosses constantly preached safety as their crews faced danger daily. Snags—burned trees still standing—could fall quietly with no warning. Chain saws and even sharp hand tools posed dangers to the weary crews. At the end of August, however, no serious injuries had been reported from the firefighting effort, despite the large buildup of forces. But there were hundreds of minor injuries and smoke-related illnesses. Breathing the smoke on the front lines was like smoking four packs of cigarettes a day.

For the crews, the day's assignment often included hours of scraping the earth bare near the fires with pulaskis—firefighting tools that are half hoe and half axe. Looking much like a hiking trail, these fire lines are designed to stop a ground fire. They were ineffective in Yellowstone, however, as the fire swept

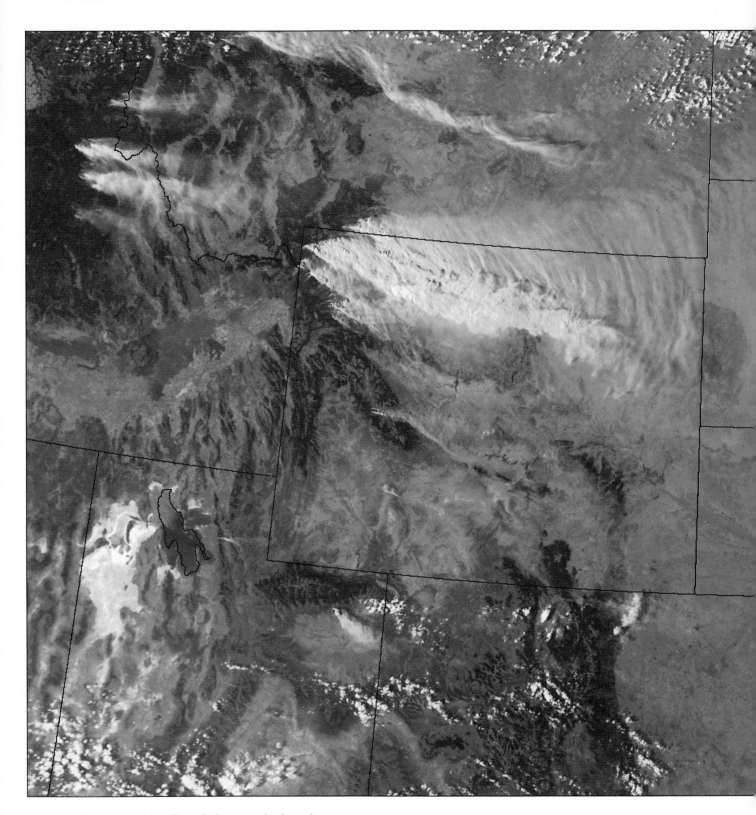

*A satellite image taken Sept. 7 shows smoke from the
Yellowstone fires drifting across northern Wyoming,
southern Montana, Nebraska, North Dakota and South
Dakota.* COURTESY USGS EROS DATA CENTER

*Above: Park employees
huddle near the Old
Faithful geyser, seeking
refuge from the
firestorm sweeping
down on the geyser
basin.* JUDY TELL

through the treetops or spotted over the lines. At one point, 400 miles of fire line were in place. When the winds came up, only 20 miles held.

The lack of success frustrated firefighters and their bosses. Poncin, the commander for the North Fork fire, had spent five weeks directing firefighters in Yellowstone. The North Fork fire grew despite his best efforts. "You don't like to walk away from a fire with the smoke column as large as when you arrived," he said.

Residents of the region also were weary of the fire and constant smoke. Despite the massive firefighting effort, they maintained the perception that the park's "let it burn" policy still was in effect. Only a halfhearted effort was being made to extinguish the blazes, they thought.

Angry residents directed their frustration directly at Yellowstone Superintendent Robert Barbee. He had held controversial posts in the Park Service before, but this was the first time he had been subjected to such extensive personal attacks, including one West Yellowstone motel marquee which said, "Welcome to the Barbee-que." Some attacks came from people who operate tourism businesses and who wondered whether tourism would recover. Others reacted emotionally to fire running rampant through the magnificent landscape that held some personal attachment.

To quell the sharp criticism, top regional directors of the National Park Service and U.S. Forest Service conducted a press conference over Labor Day weekend to explain the extreme fire conditions and the efforts to stop the fires. They also carried another message—another dry cold front was forecast. That would mean that another quarter million acres could burn in Yellowstone in the next three days. Their predictions soon became reality.

The fire season climaxed during the first 10 days of September. Rampant flames swept across the landscape, so wide and full that avoiding towns and buildings seemed impossible. Flames swept up to, around or over nearly every development inside Yellowstone and threatened communities just outside its boundaries.

The Clover-Mist fire, 25 miles wide and 30 miles long, swept down drainages toward cabins and ranches tucked into the forest in the Crandall Creek and Sunlight Basin areas east of the park. Downslope

winds blew the North Fork fire two miles toward West Yellowstone on the night of Sept. 1, throwing an eerie orange glow in the sky above the town. Residents filled their cars with gasoline, loaded valuables and prepared to flee. The fire stopped a mile and a quarter from town.

Fire crews manning engines, many from volunteer fire departments throughout Montana and Wyoming, were assigned to protect towns and buildings from the onslaught.

On Sept. 1, a firefighter described the Storm Creek fire northeast of Yellowstone as "burning like a freight train at 9 p.m.," as it chugged toward Cooke City and Silver Gate. Two days later, the fire roared through the historic Silvertip Ranch, an exclusive, private guest ranch along Yellowstone's northern boundary. Three dozen firefighters deployed fire shelters as the blaze swept past them. Remarkably, there were no injuries and no buildings burned.

In the path of the Storm Creek fire, Cooke City and Silver Gate residents were evacuated. Bulldozers gashed a huge fire line through the forest near Yellowstone's northeast entrance in an effort to stop the blaze.

Fire bosses decided to defend the towns by waiting for favorable winds, then lighting a backfire. They calculated that a backfire would burn toward the Storm Creek fire and scorch an area that would starve the advancing inferno. Without the backburn, they feared that the Storm Creek fire could roar through the communities.

The backfire was lit and watched for two days. Then the wind shifted and an ember from the backfire crossed the bulldozed fire line. The wind whipped the small spot fire into a wall of flame that swept toward Silver Gate. The fire later moved north of Silver Gate and Cooke City, spreading east toward Cooke Pass and destroying several homes and cabins. Ironically, the Storm Creek fire never burned into the backfire.

Above: Denny Bungarz,
fire boss of the North
Fork fire, conducts a
tour of the park for
Interior Secretary
Donald Hodel, right,
and Wyoming Governor
Mike Sullivan.
LARRY MAYER

On Sept. 6, the perimeters of the Yellowstone area fires exceeded 1 million acres and they still raged out of control. "Mother Nature is making the decisions here," one spokeswoman said.

Gary Cargill, the U.S. Forest Service's Rocky Mountain regional forester, applauded the efforts of firefighters, despite the disappointments. "They are crack firefighters who are not used to getting whipped day after day."

The firefighting effort had swollen to 9,500 people and 117 aircraft, including the Army's huge Chinook helicopters. Eleven of the nation's most experienced fire-management teams supervised the 13 named fires in the Yellowstone area. Fire danger grew so extreme in Montana that the governor banned all outdoor recreation. Smoke continued to pour out of the park, exceeding healthy levels in many gateway communities.

Meanwhile, the threat to Old Faithful loomed again. Fire that had slopped over a month-old containment line on the southern tip of the North Fork fire had marched seven miles and was within a mile of Old Faithful on the night of Sept. 6. Park officials decided to evacuate the 700 guests at the historic Old Faithful Inn the next morning. Bellhops knocked on doors and asked guests to leave in an orderly evacuation.

The fire burned closer throughout the next morning and early afternoon, separated from the historic geyser basin and 400-building town by only a low ridge. A huge smoke column billowed over the development as a steady stream of air tankers dropped retardant on the leading edge of the fire and helicopters dipped water buckets from a sewage treatment lagoon that had been filled with fresh water.

In midafternoon, winds picked up and the fire crested the ridge a quarter of a mile from Old Faithful.

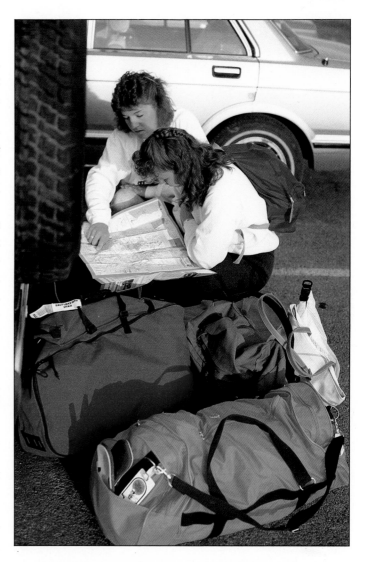

Right: A pair of tourists studies a road map after being forced to evacuate the Old Faithful Inn. The historic inn was not damaged by fire.
BOB ZELLAR

Next page: Flames consume one of the 16 buildings destroyed when the North Fork fire overran the Old Faithful complex. Most of the buildings were small cabins.
ROBERT EKEY

Heat radiated to the parking lot. Tourists and concessionaire employees still in the area, some approaching hysteria, were shepherded from the area by a park ranger in a patrol car.

Suddenly the wind shifted and strengthened and the fierce firestorm swept down onto Old Faithful in a matter of minutes. Firefighters assigned to protect government housing on the edge of the village had to retreat hastily from the flames. Wind blew thick, brown smoke into the village and sent glowing embers the size of golf balls skidding across the pavement.

Firestorms have rolling action, burning so intensely that the heat alone can set a building on fire. At Old Faithful, as the fire rolled in, flying embers landed on building roofs. Sixteen small cabins and a storage shed burned as firefighters dashed around the development trying to put out small fires. A deluge system was activated on the Old Faithful Inn, wetting the roof

and saving the historic log hotel from being damaged. Denny Bungarz, the North Fork fire boss who often offered an optimistic outlook, got a fire shelter out of the trunk of his car during the height of the firestorm.

An ember, which apparently had flown over the village and geyser basin, landed on a hillside half a mile from the nearest fire and ignited the forest. Within a minute it swept 100 yards through the timber.

Ken Dittmer, commander for all of the fires in the Yellowstone area, said later that a wind shift of 2 or 3 degrees to the south could have meant disaster for the entire village, including the inn. "No amount of engines or water would have made any difference. We were right on the ragged edge," he said.

Bungarz said that Old Faithful no longer was threatened by the North Fork fire—it already had burned around the area—but that the fire had thwarted all efforts to stop or slow it. "We threw everything at that fire from Day One," he said. "We tried everything we knew of or could think of, and that fire kicked our ass from one end of the park to the other."

Left: A seemingly endless stream of firefighters marches to the front lines of the Clover-Mist fire. Thousands of firefighters battled the 387,000-acre fire.
BOB ZELLAR

Above: A U.S. Marine from Camp Pendleton, Calif., surveys the fire scene near Mammoth. Toward the end of the Yellowstone firefighting effort, troops relieved civilian fire crews.
LARRY MAYER

Right: Cooke City residents gather to listen to Park Service reports about fires approaching their mountain community.
LARRY MAYER

The same day saw intense fire activity in other areas. The Clover-Mist fire burned 13 mobile homes and a store in the Crandall Creek area east of Yellowstone, where 50 homes had been evacuated. Four buildings

Left: Despite widespread fires, many tourists carried on normal activities, including fishing in the Firehole River while fires burn on the opposite bank.
LARRY MAYER

Above: Fire on the hillside behind Cooke City threatened to engulf the gateway community.
JAMES WOODCOCK

were burned in Cooke Pass, victims of the backfire which raged out of control. The Wolf Lake fire sent embers into Canyon Village and started a major run toward Mammoth and the park's headquarters. The threat to other towns had decreased as the fires swept around them. Protecting Mammoth, home to many park employees, became a priority.

As the fires raged, President Ronald Reagan sent members of his cabinet to Yellowstone on a fact-finding mission. Interior Secretary Donald Hodel, Agriculture Secretary Richard Lyng and Undersecretary of Defense William Taft arrived with the park and the region under siege by the massive fires. Five communities along the park boundaries were evacuated and fire still burned on the outskirts of nearly every development inside the park. The cabinet officers said they were shocked

by the extent of the fires. They promised more help from the military and a review of the Park Service and Forest Service fire-management policy.

The firefighting effort was costing $3 million a day and already had totaled $89 million.

When the cabinet officials arrived on Sept. 11, there was another arrival—the first significant rain since July. The next morning, snow blanketed the park with a dusting in some areas and ankle-deep in others. Firefighters finally got the break they had hoped for all summer.

For the next week, light precipitation fell on-and-off in the region, slowing the fires. U.S. Marines arrived to help with the effort. The end, it seemed, was near. But officials characterized the fires as sleeping giants that could spring back to life if the rain stopped.

Democratic presidential candidate Michael Dukakis visited the park on Sept. 16, trying to capitalize on the national attention given to the fires. Hundreds of reporters now covered the fires, in turn attracting a procession of VIPs who took fire bosses away from the fire lines for briefings.

Fall was coming to the high country and, with it, moisture and cooler temperatures which slowed the fires. On Sept. 17, fire commanders cautiously said they had turned the corner on the Yellowstone fires. For the first time in two months, talk turned to containing the blazes.

The firefighting effort tapered off quickly as crews, mostly military, worked to mop up hot spots. Of 5,500 firefighters in the region, 4,000 were army infantrymen or marines. Crews found themselves in the ironic situation of fighting to keep warm in light snow and cold

Above: A volunteer fire department truck stands by to protect a building in Silver Gate as the Storm Creek fire rages north of town.
JAMES WOODCOCK

Right: Old Faithful geyser erupts against a smoke cloud hours before a firestorm swept through the area.
BOB ZELLAR

rain while fighting forest fires. The fires continued to smolder on dry days, but daily advances were small.

Though safety continued to be a priority, the fires took their first life in September, killing a firefighter with a falling snag during mop-up operations. A second snag seriously injured another firefighter, and a pilot

escaped injury when his helicopter crashed upside down in a lake east of Yellowstone.

Firefighters worked into late October mopping up the fires, while other crews started rehabilitation of areas scarred by firefighting. Fire crews doused the last fires in late October, ending three months of battle.

Early estimates show that 900,000 acres—about 40 percent—of Yellowstone National Park were touched by fire. About 1.3 million acres burned in the Yellowstone region. In about a third of the burned-over area, trees were untouched. Those areas would turn green in the spring.

In the greater Yellowstone area, the fires burned 3 houses, 13 mobile homes, 10 private cabins, 2 Forest Service cabins, a Park Service cabin and 18 cabins in Yellowstone that were leased or owned by the park's concessionaire.

During the $120 million effort, firefighters dug

Above: Soldiers build a fire line near Old Faithful in one of many futile attempts to stop the fires. JUDY TELL

Right: Marines hike along the Gardner River after a day on the fire lines near Mammoth.
LARRY MAYER

Above: Firefighters light backfires near the park's northeast entrance as they try to burn up fuel in the path of an approaching blaze. BOB ZELLAR

Right: Soldiers crowd around a camp stove as the first snow of the year falls on the park. The September snowfall marked the beginning of the end of the fire season. LARRY MAYER

more than 850 miles of fire line by hand. Some 600 miles of that was around the North Fork fire. Bulldozers scraped an additional 137 miles of fire lines, including 32 miles in Yellowstone. More than 1.4 million gallons of retardant were dropped from aerial tankers, and helicopters dropped an estimated 10 million gallons of water. More than 18,000 hours of aircraft time were logged over the park.

As the fall storms washed the skies clear of the dreary smoke which had hung over the region for most of the late summer, park vistas began to reappear and Yellowstone seemed a much different place. Fall colors mixed with the blackened forests in a vivid contrast. The pessimistic mood that had prevailed in the region turned to optimism.

From a tourist's point of view, most of the fire damage is in the backcountry, out of sight of roads. Driving through constant blackened forest is rare. The fires, instead, left a mosaic of black and green.

When the smoke was thick, it was difficult to assess the fire's damage. As the smoke cleared, people saw that it was not as bad as they had feared.

Many businesses in gateway communities made up what they may have lost in tourist trade by catering to firefighters. They also saw the need to spread the word that Yellowstone was not devastated. There had been extensive burning, but the fires had not affected the geysers or wildlife, the major attractions in the park.

Yellowstone's landscape began to renew itself, and the healing process seemed to extend to the residents of the region as well.

Above: Snow covers a rural volunteer fireman and his convertible truck at Mammoth. The snow was a sign that soon he would be driving his truck home.
BOB ZELLAR

Next page: A military C-130 tanker drops retardant on the North Fork fire. A total of 1.4 million gallons of retardant were dropped on the Yellowstone fires. LARRY MAYER

POLICY AND POLITICS

While forest fires raged across the Yellowstone region, another firestorm spread from the Northern Rockies to Washington, D.C.—the debate over the National Park Service's "let it burn" policy. Fueled partly by misperceptions about the policy and its effect on the Yellowstone situation, people and politicians attacked the policy and the bureaucrats who administered it.

Some of the fires that started in Yellowstone Park were allowed to burn for weeks under the "let it burn" policy and grew to massive proportions. Although Yellowstone's policy took most of the blame, fires that started outside the park accounted for 60 percent of the acres burned in the Yellowstone region.

For decades the public has been exposed to Smokey the Bear and the philosophy that all forest fires are bad. But, in the early 1970s, the federal government expanded its policy to reflect fire's vital role in the forest cycle. Smokey was relegated to snuffing man-caused fires, while federal agencies allowed some lightning-caused wilderness fires to burn so the forest could regenerate itself.

That dovetailed with the park's relatively new philosophy of "natural regulation," which was an outgrowth of a 1960s commission appointed to study the role of national parks. In the so-called Leopold Report, the commission called for reducing man's influence in the parks to preserve a vignette of primitive America.

The new doctrine, nicknamed "The Great Experiment," meant that park managers would no longer cull herds of wildlife, extinguish some lightning-caused fires or feed garbage to bears, which would be left to seek

A spectacular sunset over Yellowstone Park ends another hectic day for firefighters. BOB ZELLAR

natural sources of food.

Adopted in 1972, Yellowstone's fire management policy dictated that some lightning-caused fires would burn as long as they did not threaten human life, developments, natural features or endangered species. Man-caused fires would be suppressed in safe, cost-effective and environmentally sensitive ways. A part of the plan that never was implemented called for the Park Service to set some fires to remove dead trees and other fire hazards. During the first 15 years of the plan, hundreds of fires were left to burn in Yellowstone, but they consumed only 34,000 acres. Most fires burned less than an acre. The largest fires burned only several thousand acres.

The U.S. Forest Service also recognized the value of fire as a natural part of the landscape and, in the 1970s, adopted a similar fire-management policy for wilderness areas, but with certain limits. Fires burning within those limits were called prescribed burns. All man-caused fires and natural fires that exceeded the limits were declared wildfires and fought.

While the Park Service and Forest Service had similar goals, implementation of their separate plans differed greatly.

Yellowstone's plan primarily considered the threat to life and property, location and the age of the forest. Park officials evaluated but did not consider as major factors scientifically derived fire-danger projections that showed as early as June 1988 that "a serious fire season" was approaching.

National forests adjacent to Yellowstone used data such as the amount of energy available to fires and the moisture content of logs to gauge burning conditions. Fire experts plugged that information, along with weather data, into computers and determined that the 1988 fire season in the Yellowstone region was starting earlier and could be more severe than normal.

Scientific analysis showed the Yellowstone

Above: Bulldozers were used sparingly inside the park during early firefighting activity. The dozers later plowed 32 miles of fire line in Yellowstone.
ROBERT EKEY

Right: Despite their criticism of fire suppression policies, area residents gave overwhelming support to the men and women battling the blazes.
JAMES WOODCOCK

region in an extreme drought by mid-June. Fire experts predicted that the drought, combined with severe burning conditions, could cause extreme fire behavior. Fire danger readings which normally appear in August began developing in June and early July.

In July, the scientific data showed that fire conditions had exceeded the limits of the Forest Service's fire management plan. That "trigger" prompted the agency to fight all new forest fires. Yellowstone Park officials did not take similar action for as long as two weeks, a time when officials admit that firefighting could have been effective.

Dan Sholly, chief ranger at Yellowstone, said park officials reviewed the fire-danger projections, but they were not remarkably different from previous years and that fire behavior was not extreme. The Yellowstone region had experienced a pattern of dry winters with moist springs and summers for seven years, and park officials expected the trend to continue. The park received nearly twice its normal amount of precipitation in May, but only 20 percent of normal in June. Although fires were burning in late June, an early July shower reduced most of them

to smoldering spots.

The number of fires in June and early July in Yellowstone was similar to the previous three years, and nearly half of those fires had gone out without suppression efforts. But the fires were bigger.

Records show that, in previous years, fire starts in June and July rarely continued burning. In 1988, more than 8,500 acres had burned by July 15, including fire activity that was intense for that time of year. During previous years most of the fire activity was in August and September. Critics said the early fire activity should have served as a warning to the Park Service.

The 1988 fire season highlighted the differences between the Yellowstone and Forest Service fire-management plans. Even differences between fire plans for the individual national forests surrounding the park became apparent. The Storm Creek fire in the Absaroka-Beartooth Wilderness north of Yellowstone, and the Mink fire in the Bridger-Teton National Forest south of the park, were allowed to burn even though the Forest Service had decided to fight all new fires. Both fires were started by lightning before the scientific data triggered suppression

orders. The Storm Creek fire, in the Custer National Forest, later threatened Cooke City, and the Mink fire burned into Yellowstone Park, then spilled over the eastern boundary onto the Shoshone National Forest.

The North Fork fire was fought from the start because it was caused by the hand of man. A person gathering firewood started the blaze on July 22 some 200 yards outside of Yellowstone's western boundary in the Targhee National Forest. Despite the early firefighting effort, it became one of the largest and most destructive fires.

The North Fork fire shifted attention from the "let it burn" policy to firefighting restrictions. By the time fire crews from the Targhee National Forest arrived, the blaze already had spread into the park. They bulldozed lines around the fire in the national forest. Firefighters also wanted to use bulldozers in the park, but they were restricted to hand tools and chain saws because that area of Yellowstone is managed as wilderness, where bulldozers are prohibited. Had the firefighters been working in a Forest Service wilderness area, even chain saws would have been prohibited.

Sholly, Yellowstone's chief ranger, said bulldozers would have scarred the land, but the fire still would have blackened both sides of any fire line during the early stages of the North Fork fire. A panel appointed to review the fire agreed. The fire burned 460 acres the first day and 1,300 acres by the end of the next day. By the end of the fourth day, the fire had grown to more than 5,000 acres and was throwing embers half a mile ahead of the fire.

Yellowstone officials were reluctant to use dozers to build fire lines early in the 1988 season, claiming that the scars left by machines would remain longer than the effects of the fire. Instead, they ordered hand lines and other "light on the land" tactics. Thirty-two miles of dozer line eventually were built inside the park as fire crews worked to protect communities along Yellowstone's boundary.

Fire bosses said the light-handed tactics made their jobs different, but not more difficult. Some fire crews,

Left: A Forest Service crew drives through Cascade Meadow chasing spot fires as the Wolf Lake fire approaches Canyon.
BOB ZELLAR

Above: Civilian Vertol helicopters were hired to help make water drops on park fires. The helicopters carry buckets capable of dropping 500 gallons of water. LARRY MAYER

*Firefighter Mark
Courson gives orders to
fire crews working
along a bulldozed fire
line near Silver Gate.*
JAMES WOODCOCK

however, said the tactics prevented them from putting the fires out. Rangers warned one California Department of Forestry crew that they would receive a ticket for driving off the roadway if they continued to drive their truck needlessly through a meadow near Canyon. The crew members said they were trained to attack fires instead of waiting for the fires to move to them, as they were told to do in Yellowstone. Fire crews were constantly reminded that a different set of values was at stake in Yellowstone.

The incident with the California crew was an exception to the norm. More frequently, park employees helped fire crews, which abided by the "light on the land" tactics. As the fires grew, the Park Service relaxed its restrictions.

Requests for major disturbances to the land, such as a bulldozer line, required the park superintendent's approval. Some were rejected. Requests for two dozer lines on the Clover-Mist fire were denied because of questionable need, including one line alongside Pelican Creek, where park officials thought the creek would stop the fires just as well. One dozer line for the Clover-Mist fire was approved but never built. The fire never reached any of the three areas.

Cooperation between park officials and fire bosses generally was excellent. Dry conditions, wind and topography—not tactics—were the biggest challenges for firefighters.

As with any situation the size of the firefighting effort in the Yellowstone region, there were problems. Fire reviews identified communications and delegation of authority as consistent problems for fire bosses, who answered to the park superintendent and forest supervisors as well as the command center at West Yellowstone. While some fire bosses traded resources freely, there were confrontations over allocation of crews and equipment.

Area commanders complained that they lacked

Left: A towering column of smoke looms over West Yellowstone, signaling yet another outbreak of fire. Smoke, fear and confusion cut deeply into the tourist trade.
LARRY MAYER

Above: With Old Faithful geyser in the background, photographers and reporters swarm around Interior Secretary Donald Hodel.
LARRY MAYER

*This crew from the
California Department
of Forestry felt that
environmental concerns
hindered firefighting
efforts.* LARRY MAYER

*Above: Jeff Munuey
looks over the debris
left when his buildings
near Cooke Pass were
destroyed by a backfire.*
JAMES WOODCOCK

authority to influence fire bosses' strategies. The week before Black Saturday, the area command center recommended that the Park Service relinquish supervision of the Clover-Mist and Red-Shoshone fires to outside fire teams. Dick Cox, a Forest Service fire specialist working as an area commander, said later that commanders thought Park Service employees directing the firefighting were spread too thin.

The Park Service had responsibility for all fires in Yellowstone except the Fan and North Fork fires. In addition, the park staff was responsible for suppressing all new fires and handling the daily operations of the park.

"Our thinking at that time was that they were scattered far too thin," Cox said. "I felt they had too much to handle. That was our concern....We felt we were far behind the power curve at that point.

"The fire chief, Dan Sholly, felt they were going to hang on to them, and that was his recommendation to [Park Superintendent Robert] Barbee," Cox said.

Sholly said that it was more efficient for the Park Service to manage the fires than to train a new management team. "Where we lost ground was in the continuity of changing overhead [fire management] teams so many times," Sholly said. Twenty-six outside fire-management teams eventually worked in the Yellowstone region—all new players who didn't know the terrain, fire behavior and the "light on the land" ethics.

Because commanders thought their hands were tied when fire bosses did not follow recommendations, the area command was given more authority in late August.

As the fire season wore on, no firefighting tactics worked. Fire swept through decades-old pine plantations, burning even an area that had burned nine years before.

"I think, given the conditions that prevailed in the summer of '88—especially late summer—no matter what man would have done there would have been big fire in Yellowstone," Barbee said. "It got to the point where if it was organic, it would burn. All the [fire behavior] models were out the window."

Barbee and all other land managers in the region said that the "let it burn" policy was not at fault. Regional Forest Service and Park Service officials said that if they regress to a policy of fighting all fires,

fuel will build up again, leading to another summer of fire.

"The longer you keep yourself protected, the more you set yourself up for cataclysm," Barbee said. "We cannot live with a situation that will burn down towns and multimillion-dollar facilities. We need some fail-safes in the system."

Forest ecologists disagree on what effect previous fire-suppression efforts had on the fuel buildup that contributed to the severity of the summer's fires. The U.S. Army patrolled the park on horses in the early part of the century, putting out fires. When the National Park Service was established in 1916, rangers took over the firefighting responsibilities. Some experts claim effective firefighting efforts were not launched until after World War II when aircraft and other machines became a regular part of the effort. If the only effective firefighting occurred between the war and the 1972 implementation of the "let it burn" policy, it would account for only 10 percent of the forest cycle, hardly enough time for a significant fuel buildup.

Other experts claim that fire suppression was effective for as long as a century. Although no machinery was available to aid early firefighters, fires could smolder for weeks—as they did in Yellowstone in 1988—and be discovered and extinguished by soldiers or rangers on horseback.

Fires not only reduce fuel buildup, but also create natural breaks in the landscape which can slow or stop later fires.

Abandoning the "let it burn" policy now would only allow fuels to build up and be expensive. The "let it burn" policy was partially justified in saving the cost of sending firefighters to every fire, though most would go out on their own.

Some experts want a fire-management policy that would allow man to ignite fires in the spring or fall—when they would burn but not get out of control—to eliminate pockets of fuel and create firebreaks. Such a proposal would have a better chance for success on national forest lands, which have more natural fire barriers, than the flat plateaus of Yellowtone. But it

---

Above: Yellowstone
Park Superintendent
Robert Barbee was the
subject of intense
criticism for the park's
"let it burn" policy.
LARRY MAYER

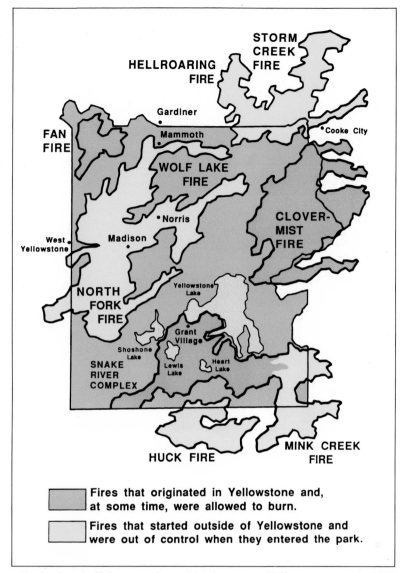

*Fewer than half the acres burned in the greater Yellowstone area in 1988
were by fires which fell under the Park Service's "let it burn" policy.*

MAP BY JOHN POTTER

also may work around developments in Yellowstone to create natural firebreaks around the buildings.

During the heat of the fires, Interior Secretary Donald Hodel said the "let it burn" policy would receive a thorough review. He would not propose changes, but said there was a clear need to modify the system that somehow had failed.

Forestry experts are confident that, over time, the natural-burn policy will remain intact, and that the importance of fire in the ecosystem will continue to be recognized. But, the Park Service and Forest Service policies are likely to become more similar, with the Park Service adopting some of the scientific "triggers" that warn of extreme burning conditions.

Some Park Service employees defend the old policy, saying the Forest Service's triggers did not work in the Storm Creek and Mink fires. A policy with triggers which are too conservative could defeat the purpose of a natural-fire policy because most fires would be extinguished, they believe.

Others argue that, despite any written fire policy, park superintendents and forest supervisors will be much more likely in the near future to douse naturally occurring fires rather than risk duplicating the Yellowstone fire experience.

The "let it burn" doctrine is not the only policy which was challenged during the Yellowstone fires. The entire philosophy of letting nature take its course was threatened as the fires peaked.

Calls for massive reforestation and revegetation programs came from a public unaware of the decades-old effort to keep Yellowstone and its surrounding wilderness areas "natural." Park officials have worked to keep only plants native to the area in the ecosystem.

Offers of pine seedlings from Georgia, New Jersey and Washington to help replant Yellowstone were well-intended, but contradicted all that Yellowstone stands for.

Some segments of the public also called for the park to feed Yellowstone's animals over the winter. Elk and bison populations were at record-high levels and their winter range was severely affected by the drought. Little of the range burned, but the sparse forage coupled with a severe winter could mean greater than average winterkill. Park officials believe that feeding animals would only delay the eventual winterkill and could lead to more disease among animals.

During the height of the blazes, people thought Yellowstone would be forever changed. Residents of gateway communities who depend upon Yellowstone for their livelihoods feared that the fires would damage tourism in the future. Attacks on the Park Service, including Superintendent Robert Barbee, were vicious and frequent. Barbee once likened the mood to a "lynch-mob, hang 'em" mentality.

"The day the smoke cleared, almost immediately the mood began to shift," Barbee said. "As the air cleared, there were amazing attitudinal changes. The anger seemed to leave and the irrationality of the whole thing disappeared. I now realize fully that when the stakes are perceived to be high, trying to hang on to the fundamental values of national parks and wilderness areas becomes more difficult."

"The set-up was perfect. We were going around happy-faced with stories about how great fire is. Then, the fires got bigger and bigger and bigger. How could it be good when it was threatening to burn down the Old Faithful Inn, a national icon?" he said.

"We need to say there is a lot of educational value here, while in no way or form celebrating this. I never would have wanted a fire like this. But, we still need to put a positive spin on this whole thing and work with the travel and tourism industry to spread the word that Yellowstone is still here," Barbee said.

Previous page: A herd of elk walks through a recently burned area along the Madison River. Fires were less damaging to elk range than the drought.
BOB ZELLAR

Above: Streams of water are sprayed on buildings in Cooke City to protect them from embers flying ahead of the rapidly approaching Storm Creek fire.

JAMES WOODCOCK

Next page: fires left forests littered with snags, standing dead trees that firefighters called "silent killers" because they fall without warning.

JAMES WOODCOCK

Rebirth Of A Forest

Yellowstone always has displayed a bizarre side, as if Mother Nature had decided this was the place to be a bit eccentric.

The 10,000 geothermal features, where the earth vents itself through the world's largest geyser basin, are evidence of Yellowstone's calamitous natural history. Through the eyes of geologists, the landscape tells us that events in the past make the 1988 summer of fires seem insignificant in Yellowstone's heritage.

A giant caldera—a bowl-shaped basin covering the heart of Yellowstone—is all that remains of a giant volcano that erupted 600,000 years ago, then collapsed into itself. Many of the park's geothermal features are found along the edges of the caldera.

Yellowstone's dynamic geology gives scientists a chance to watch the slow-motion changes in the earth's shape, rather than just interpreting evidence from the past. Yellowstone Lake is slowly tilting to the south, flooding the southern arms and cutting off its flow into the Yellowstone River to the north.

One of the world's most diverse and bountiful petrified forests stands in the Yellowstone area. Trees buried by mudslides eons ago display a landscape once so diverse that it was host to trees ranging from subalpine to subtropical. In those times, elevations varied by 10,000 feet, similar to areas of South America today.

The volcanic activity and uplifting raised the elevations in the area. But much of that land has eroded or been sculpted by glaciers. When the glaciers retreated northward 12,000 years ago, the climate conditions

Fire is part of the natural cycle of the forest and is just as important as rain and sun in promoting regeneration. New plant growth helps improve wildlife habitat

LARRY MAYER

| OVERMATURE FOREST | FIRE | 0-60 YEARS | 60-150 YEARS | 150-300 YEARS | 300-400 YEARS |

Yellowstone's lodgepole forests have a 250-to-400-year cycle, which ends with fire. After the fire, ground cover and lodgepole seedlings sprout on the forest floor, creating thousands of new trees. The lodgepoles thin themselves out over centuries, eventually yielding to spruce and fir trees. Lightning often starts fires in what is classified as an "overmature" lodgepole forest. ART BY JOHN POTTER

and topography dictated the type of vegetation that now survives in Yellowstone. High elevations and harsh winters translate into short growing seasons, and plants and animals that have adapted to them.

Fire has been a part of that landscape ever since the glaciers receded—ever since there was vegetation to burn. Fire is as natural as sunshine, snow and rain in these forests. It is the agent by which the forest renews itself. Fire is so established that many of the plants have evolved to adapt to it, including lodgepole pines, whose cones pop open under intense heat.

Yellowstone forests started renewing themselves within weeks of the fires. New ground cover sprouting in moist areas and thousands of pine seedlings appeared on each acre of charred land. The rate of recovery will depend on the intensity of the fire.

Of the 1.3 million acres that burned in the Yellowstone area, 900,000 are in the national park. About 58 percent of the burned area was charred by canopy burns—where the treetops burned, leaving only scorched trunks standing amidst blackened soil. In most of those areas, heat did not penetrate more than an inch into the soil, allowing roots and bulbs to survive. Those underground remains will sprout grasses and wildflowers in spring to compete with thousands of lodgepole pines per acre.

Fewer than 10,000 acres burned severely—where

the soil baked for days and was sterilized. Those areas usually had logs several inches off the ground that burned for days. Areas which produced the most dramatic sights—those resembling a barren moonscape—actually sustained only moderate damage, and regeneration is expected to appear within a year. In the sterilized areas, regeneration may not occur for a decade.

In about 37 percent of the burned areas, flames never reached the treetops. In those areas, the ground will green, leaving scorched tree trunks as the only evidence of the summer of fire.

In the meadows, grasslands and sagebrush, grasses will grow back greener the next year, improving forage for wildlife.

Right: Amid the chaos of the summer of fires, the Firehole River appears tranquil and serene as it winds its way toward the Madison River.
BOB ZELLAR

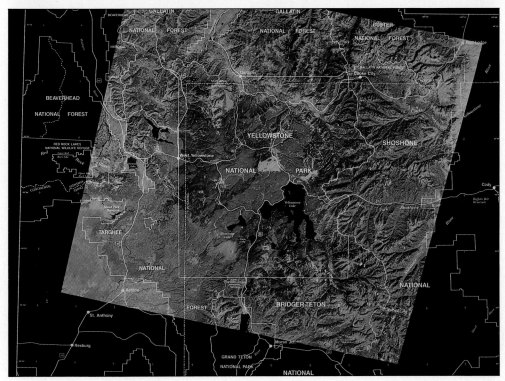

*Left: An elk calf returns
to the burned forest.*
BOB ZELLAR

*Top: Intense heat from
forest fires causes
lodgepole cones to pop
open and release their
seeds. Some of the
seeds will sprout, while
others provide food for
squirrels and mice.*
BOB ZELLAR

*Bottom: A computer-
generated image taken
by a LANDSAT satellite
in October shows the
burned areas of
Yellowstone in red.*
COURTESY USGS EROS
DATA CENTER

*As the fires began
to die down, army
troops and marines
supplemented civilian
fire crews.*
LARRY MAYER

Historians speculate that Native Americans used fire centuries ago to renew grasslands and improve wildlife habitat. They disagree, however, on whether Indians ignited the forests. The prevailing theory is that they burned areas in the forests only for trails and campsites.

The forests themselves hint that massive burns have occurred in the Yellowstone area in the past. Researchers have found evidence of large fires in the 1750s and 1780s. As many as 800,000 acres may have burned then, according to Don Despain, a Yellowstone plant ecologist who specializes in fire.

Speaking from a strictly ecological view, biologists say that fire is neither good nor bad. The cycle of the forest includes fire as much in its scheme as it does the four seasons. "If we can take all the people out of the ecosystem and look at it from a purely ecological standpoint, fire is a perfectly natural, normal event, just like rain and snow. It's a rare event, but it has happened many times already," Despain said.

Historically, 80 percent of lightning-caused fires begin in overmature lodgepole forests littered with downed trees and decades worth of fallen pine needles. Spruce and fir trees slowly squeeze out the lodgepoles on their way to becoming the dominant species. The

Above: Animals in the park were usually undisturbed by the firefighting activity.
LARRY MAYER

Right: Some deer, elk and moose were trapped in quickly moving firestorms and killed. JAMES WOODCOCK

Next page: A National Park Service photographer walks across an area near Canyon where fire swept through acres of blown-down trees.
LARRY MAYER

fire starts on the ground, feeding on wood left from when the lodgepoles dominated the forest. The shorter spruce and fir trees act as ladders and carry flames to the tops of the taller lodgepoles, where they burn the canopy.

Ash is one of fire's most important by-products. Elk and moose often move into a burned area within days of a fire for the minerals found in the ash. Rain and snow help break the ash down into nutrients that percolate back into the soil.

The nutrients foster abundant plant growth the next year. The forest floor fills with elk sedge and heartleaf arnica. Fireweed, western meadowrue, aster and grouse whortleberry thrive.

Immediately after a fire, 50,000 to 100,000 lodgepole pine cones per acre burst open and release their seeds. In the fertile soil, the seeds sprout and, within three years, grow 8 inches with needles 2 to 3 inches long. Three-year-old seedlings in unburned areas grow at less than half that rate. Mice, squirrels and birds eat many of the seeds, but within five years, as many as 1,000 seedlings per acre remain.

The growth rate of a forest depends on many factors, especially moisture and exposure to sunlight. During the first 30 to 60 years, lodgepoles grow to 12 to 15 feet tall and are a couple of inches in diameter. Foresters call this stage of rebirth a "doghair forest" because the trees appear to be as thick as the hair on a dog's hide. During this part of the rebirth, lodgepoles start to squeeze themselves until their population drops to only 500 trees per acre.

During the next 150 to 200 years, lodgepoles reach 6 to 8 inches in diameter and 30 to 40 feet in height. Competition for light and water thins them to 200 to 300 per acre. Grouse whortleberry bushes dominate the ground, and spruce and fir seedlings appear and grow to be several feet tall.

Spruce and fir grow to a height of 6 to 8 feet over the next 50 to 100 years, largely on the strength of water and light stolen from their lodgepole neighbors. The competition means that more lodgepoles die and fall to the ground.

During the last 100 years of the forest cycle, spruce and fir catch up to the height of the lodgepoles, which continue to perish. Without fire, spruce and fir trees would dominate the forests. But fire strikes too frequently—especially during the final century of the

forest's cycle, when fuel litters the forest floor.

Wildlife has adapted to the evolution of the forest. During the 1988 fires, elk and bison often stood within several hundred yards of the flames, nonchalantly grazing in meadows.

Record numbers of hawks rode thermals in front of the fires. In the Hayden Valley, which carries the Yellowstone River northward out of Yellowstone Lake, biologists usually see only one or two prairie hawks each year. When forest fires were burning, they saw as many as 40 in one day. Biologists speculated that the hawks were drawn to the fire by the smoke columns, then caught a free ride on the thermal currents while they searched the ground for small animals whose cover had burned.

While most larger animals, such as elk and bison,

Left: Charred trees stand in stark contrast against the clear, blue skies of Yellowstone. JAMES WOODCOCK

Above: Trumpeter swans glide across the Madison River. Oblivious to all the fire activity around them, this pair stayed in the area throughout the summer. BOB ZELLAR

easily avoided the flames, some fell in fast-moving firestorms. In Yellowstone Park, fire or smoke inhalation killed 254 large mammals, including 243 elk, 4 deer, 2 moose and 5 bison. The park is home to between 30,000 and 35,000 elk and 2,700 bison.

Other animals which died during the fires included surface-dwelling insects, small mammals and some birds which had not yet fledged. Soil-dwelling insects such as ants and beetles often were not affected.

As soon as fire swept through an area, insects invaded the burned forest to feed on standing dead trees. Woodpeckers followed. Other birds and squirrels grabbed pine seeds.

The philosophy of nature dictates that, in a purely biological sense, fire is neither an absolute detriment nor benefit. Fire destroys habitat for a red squirrel, but creates new grazing grounds for elk. Elk killed by fire provide carrion for grizzly bears during the time of year when their appetites are greatest as they prepare for hibernation.

Fire keeps the strongest plants in check and ensures that other species thrive, at least for a while. The fires

*Left: Blackened trees
bear witness to the
intensity of the fires
along the Firehole
River, but such blazes
are part of nature's
eternal cycle.*

LARRY MAYER

enhanced Yellowstone's ecological diversity by leaving a mosaic of green, brown and blackened areas inside the fire perimeters. Fire spotting left blackened islands, surrounded by heat-browned vegetation and green, unburned areas that provide wildlife with habitat in several ages of forest.

As the fires died, park officials and foresters assessed the damage and recommended rehabilitation work needed before snow blanketed the area.

Thousands of acres had been scarred by fire lines, fire camps and heliports. Some steep backcountry slopes, where vegetation was burned off, threatened to fill streams with sediment during spring runoff.

In the aftermath of the fires, more water will leave the Yellowstone ecosystem as liquid. There are fewer trees and other plants to absorb water and release it through their leaves and needles as vapor. Less plant cover also will mean less shade and accelerated spring runoff of the snowpack.

For Yellowstone's world-famous trout population, the increased runoff could muddy the water. But sand in the water also will scour the creek bottoms and create new spawning areas. New plant growth along streams will mean more food for the trout.

Crews also placed more than 500 small log dams across streams in Yellowstone's backcountry to trap sediment during spring runoff.

As part of the multimillion-dollar rehabilitation effort in Yellowstone Park, crews removed snags that posed danger to the public. Area residents cut firewood from along roadways to eliminate the hazard.

Foresters planted annual grasses along fire lines throughout the Yellowstone area to check the expected erosion. The grasses, such as rye, were selected because they will live for one or two seasons, then yield to native grasses and wildflowers.

In the Gallatin and Shoshone national forests north and east of Yellowstone, helicopters dropped tons of the grass seeds on steep slopes and along waterways.

Yellowstone Park ordered no seeding in areas other than those scarred by firefighting. A blue-ribbon panel of independent scientists recommended against seeding in the backcountry, saying the areas will regenerate on their own. Seeding could slow natural regeneration by starting grasses that would compete with native plants, according to Norman Christensen, a Duke University forest ecology professor who chaired the committee. Seeding also could increase the risk of introducing noxious weeds.

The panel also recommended against planting trees in the park or wilderness areas. Reforestation is an expensive operation and does not take into account the subtle differences in strains of species that have evolved to allow themselves the best chance of survival in the area. The panel said that some burned areas of the national forests, which are managed for timber, could be replanted, although such proposals should be carefully studied.

"There is a natural tendency to think we should do something," Christensen said. "But, in these areas the system can do just fine on its own, thank you."

Crews in Yellowstone planted some trees to hide firefighting scars, but park officials said the work resembled landscaping more than massive reforestation.

Yellowstone's wildness, special features and dynamic geology have provided a natural laboratory for hundreds of scientists. The research effort following the fires will be unparalleled, giving the scientific community a rare opportunity to chronicle and interpret how nature restores itself.

Part of the recovery effort will focus on educating the public on the natural role of fire in ecosystems. The Park Service plans to work with adjacent national forests to develop programs for tourists to explain fire ecology. Program plans include parking lots near burned areas with displays explaining how the fire swept through the area and how regeneration is taking place. The education program also will include videos and brochures.

Park officials want to convince tourists that Yellowstone is alive and well and worth visiting. Tourism has increased at sites of other major natural events, such as the volcano at Mount St. Helens in Washington. Part of the message to tourists is that, when fire is considered in the context of the calamitous changes in Yellowstone over millennia, it is a superficial event.

Yellowstone was scorched by fire and, for some people, it semed a disaster. Raging flames threatened communities and endangered firefighters. Some magnificent places in the landscape—dear to the hearts of many—are changed for our generation and generations to follow.

But through Yellowstone's rich geology, we can see that nature operates in a spectrum far different from our own. The fires in Yellowstone provide us with an opportunity to witness nature's long view of the landscape.

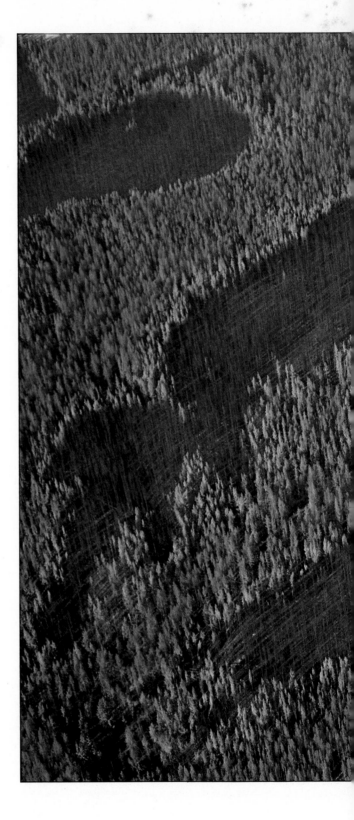

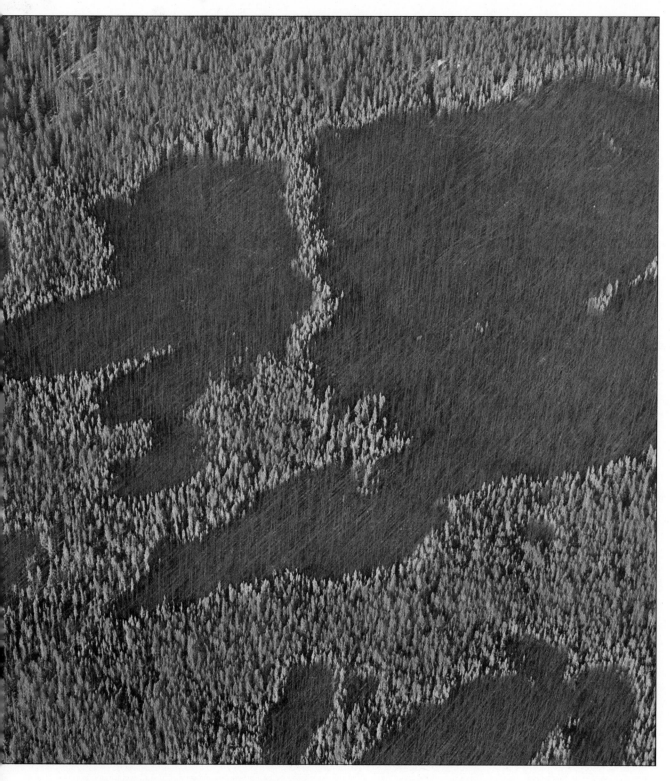

Above: Spot fires leave blackened areas as varied in shape as clouds in the sky. This photo shows the spotting activity on the North Fork fire. LARRY MAYER

Next page: Grass sprouts several weeks after fire charred the area near Grant Village. LARRY MAYER

ABOUT THE AUTHOR AND THE PHOTOGRAPHERS

DAVID SCOTT SMITH

Robert Ekey joined the staff of *The Billings Gazette* in 1984, operating its bureau in Bozeman. Yellowstone National Park is part of his regular beat. He is a graduate of the Ohio University School of Journalism and worked for daily newspapers in Ohio for 10 years before moving to Montana. His stories have also appeared in *Business Week* and Reuters, an international news service.

TOM HOWARD

James Woodcock was a freelance photographer before joining the staff of *The Billings Gazette* in 1985. He has a degree in communications from Eastern Montana College. His work has appeared in *Business Week, Audubon, Country* and *News Photographer*. He, his wife, Marybeth, and son, Tanner, reside in Billings.

DAVID SCOTT SMITH

Larry Mayer, chief photographer for *The Billings Gazette,* joined the *Gazette* staff in 1977. His work has appeared in the *New York Times, Time, Newsweek, U.S. News and World Report, American West,* Associated Press, United Press International and *National Wildlife.* Born in Livingston, Mont., he now lives in Billings with his wife, Joyce, and children Eric and Alec.

LARRY MAYER

Judy Tell began her photojournalism career in 1977 and joined *The Billings Gazette* staff in 1985. She has a degree in English literature from Michigan State University and is secretary of the National Press Photographers Association. She lives in Billings with her husband, Jeff Nies, and children Ashley and Carter. Her work has appeared in the *Chicago Tribune, Milwaukee Journal* and the Associated Press.

LARRY MAYER

Bob Zellar started his career in photojournalism in Minnesota in 1976 and joined the staff of *The Billings Gazette* in 1980. He studied photojournalism at the University of Minnesota. His work has appeared in *U.S. News and World Report* and the Associated Press. He and his wife, Pat, live in Billings.